12·6·78

MAN WITH A SONG

Some Major & Minor Notes
In the Life of

FRANCIS OF ASSISI

MAN WITH A SONG

Some Major & Minor Notes
In the Life of

FRANCIS OF ASSISI

By
FRANCIS RAYMOND LINE
and
HELEN E. LINE

FRANCISCAN HERALD PRESS
1434 WEST 51st STREET
CHICAGO, ILLINOIS 60609

Line, Francis R
  Man with a song.

1. Francesco d'Assisi, Saint, 1182-1226.
2. Christian saints—Italy—Assisi—Biography.
3. Assisi—Biography. I. Line, Helen E., joint author.
II. Title.
BX4700.F6L548   271'.3'024(B)   79-15316
ISBN 0-8199-0756-1

Certain portions of the text originally appeared in **Alive Now!**, May-June, 1977 and appear with permission of the editor.

Text on pages 109-110 is from "The Historical Roots of Our Ecologic Crisis," White, L., Jr., **Science**, Vol. 155, pp. 1203-1207, 10 March 1967 and appears with permission of the publication and author.

ALL PHOTOGRAPHS IN THIS BOOK ARE BY HELEN E. LINE

To
Dr. Maxie Dunnam
World Editor of The Upper Room
who encouraged us to write about
St. Francis
and to
Dr. Gary Herbertson,
Senior Information Officer
United Nations Environment Programme
who encouraged us in the making
of an educational motion picture
on St. Francis' life.

FOREWORD

This beautifully visioned book flows like some streams in the High Sierra: rapidly, cleanly, joyously — as if going somewhere. Which it most emphatically is. For its theme is that irrepressible singer of life's wonder and urgency, the brown-robed Francis of Assisi, who asked himself, "What am I here for, if not to lift people's hearts to spiritual joy?"

The collaborating authors, Helen and Francis Line, have earned the right to share their enthusiasm for their favorite saint. This husband and wife team has caught the spirit of St. Francis because they were imbued with his spirit long before they started writing. This is a book which has not so much been written, as it has been **lived.** For much of their lives, Helen and Francis have attempted to follow in St. Francis' footsteps — leading lifestyles of simplicity, cherishing and responding to God's natural world, extending helping hands of love and joy to people who come to them for counsel and refreshment of spirit.

They love the earth much as Francis of Assisi did. To celebrate their last wedding anniversary they hiked down to the bottom of the Grand Canyon in a snow blizzard, then up again — 21 miles of strenuous grandeur and joy.

Their home is a rendezvous for people who come on retreat and for wildlife that comes for shelter. In recent years hundreds — perhaps thousands — of birds, both local and migratory, have feasted during the day on the seeds regularly provided in their garden with its life-size wood hewn statue of St. Francis, while families of 'possums, skunks, and raccoons have come to visit by night.

The Lines' home is a place where you become whole again after a few hours of looking out at the ever-changing ocean and the feathered passersby, then at the varied evening visitors.

How the beloved little man of Assisi would have reveled in that scene! Where even various hawks float by on occasion to see if they can discover what the secret is.

More than we may suspect, our enemy today is heaviness, or solemnity — crisis following crisis, wars and rumors of wars. Francis of Assisi understood the absurdity of conflicts and violence, for he had experienced war and imprisonment. He pointed to a happier and more practical way. The exuberance and rhythm of that way, these daring biographers have somehow caught. It won't require us to wash the bodies of lepers or rebuild a crumbling church with our bare hands, as St. Francis did, but it could awaken us to the secret music within, which we had not realized was there all the while. This book radiantly relates a timeless man to our times.

Helen and Francis' **Man With A Song** is a celebration of life. It will start you singing.

DR. ALLAN A. HUNTER
Claremont, California

CONTENTS

St. Francis statue by Frances Rich, at St. Margaret's Episcopal Church, Palm Desert, California.

THIS IS THE MAN

A Saint for the Ages

Strange that a 13th century friar — lacking nobility of birth, formal learning, or wealth — should spread a burning influence over much of the civilized world.

Strange that this simple man should so dominate his Age in such multiple spheres of living, that he shines like a many-faceted diamond, each facet gleaming with such brilliance that the totality places him, inevitably, among God's nobility.

As a religious zealot, and itinerant preacher, Francis of Assisi saved souls with the sweep of a 20th century evangelist.

As a worshipper of the Babe of Bethlehem, he recreated Christ's birth scene and gave origin — and immortality — to the Christmas Crib.

As a lover of animals and birds and all nature, he became a forerunner of Schweitzer, and a confidant of the living creatures which he encountered.

He was a lover in a more magnificent sense. His caring for the beautiful Clare of Assisi, co-founder with him of the Order of Poor Clares, was physical and real, yet he was able to sublimate it into a relationship that makes it one of history's most poignant yet beautiful love stories.

As a social worker, he probably helped bring about the "Magna Carta" of Assisi, in which the noblemen and middle-class people of the town ended their feud and settled their longstanding differences — five years before the Magna Carta of England.

As a leader of men and women, he founded and inspired the three great religious Orders — Franciscans, Poor Clares, and an Order embracing whole families — that spread his influence throughout the nations.

Francis of Assisi, not because of erudition but out of the inspiration of a living experience that welled up from the depths of his Creator-tuned soul, gave to the world the poem and song that heralded the great age of Italian poetic literature. He foreshadowed Dante who, born two generations after Francis, said of him that he rose like a sun, to illumine everything with his rays, so that "his good influence began to bless the earth."

(*Divine Comedy, Paradiso xi 50*).

The panorama of St. Francis' life, from his companionship with birds and animals to his mystic experience of the stigmata, inspired the artists who gave birth to a new flowering of artistic expression, on canvas and altarpieces, in wood and bronze and marble.

Not only his influence but his very name in Spanish, English, and French, became imprinted across North and South America and the islands of the seas.

As the first true ecologist of Christendom, he created the needed new theology to save, not only souls, but perhaps all of 21st Century humanity.

Even in death, at age 44, St. Francis hurled a message to future generations, singing with almost his last breath a final verse to his great Canticle — a stanza enunciating his concept of this universal adventure of mortals.

Francis of Assisi was a very special creation of God —

A SAINT FOR THE AGES.

THIS IS HIS SONG

The Canticle of Brother Sun

Most high, almighty, and good Lord,
Yours is the praise, the glory, honor, blessing all.
To you, Most High, alone of right they do belong,
And no mortal man is fit to mention you.

Be praised, my Lord, of all your creature world,
And first of all Sir Brother Sun,
Who brings the day, and light you give to us through him,
And beautiful is he, agleam with mighty splendor:
Of you, Most High, he gives us indication.

Be praised, my Lord, through Sisters Moon and Stars:
In the heavens you have formed them, bright and fair and precious.

Be praised, my Lord, through Brother Wind,
Through Air, and cloudy, clear, and every kind of Weather,
By whom you give your creatures sustenance.

Be praised, my Lord, through Sister Water,
For greatly useful, lowly, precious, chaste is she.

Be praised, my Lord, through Brother Fire,
Through whom you brighten up the night,

And fair he is, and gay, and vigorous, and strong.

Be praised, O Lord, through our sister Mother Earth,
For she sustains and guides our life,
And yields us divers fruits, with tinted flowers, and grass.

Be praised, my Lord, through those who pardon give for love of you,
And bear infirmity and tribulation:
Blessed they who suffer it in peace,
For of you, Most High, they shall be crowned.

Be praised, my Lord, through our Brother Death of Body,
From whom no man among the living can escape.
Woe to those who in mortal sins will die;
Blessed those whom he will find in your most holy graces,
For the second death will do no harm to them.

Praise and bless my Lord, and thank him too,
And serve him all, in great humility.

PRELUDE

Our purpose in this book, rather than presenting details and minutia concerning Francis of Assisi, is to look behind and beyond the established record of his life into his feelings and emotions — his love of God, his caring for nature and for persons, his imitation of Christ, his lifestyle of simplicity, his contagious gladness of heart.

Three and a half centuries before Shakespeare, this spirited and spiritual genius of Assisi not only found "tongues in trees" and "sermons in stones" but discovered brotherhood in the wind and weather, sisterhood in the water and moon and stars, familyhood in all of humanity and creation. He sensed the diety in every dawning, and found a song in every sunset. His was a spirit of joy which set all the world to music. The plan and structure of this book, from Prelude to Postlude, is that of a musical composition, which Francis' whole existence resembled.

As lifelong admirers of St. Francis — one of us a namesake of his — we wish to share some of the resplendent minor and major notes of his life which have had deep meaning for us.

Our purpose is not to write a biography, but to orchestrate a life.

FRANCIS and HELEN LINE
Capistrano Beach, California

TUNED
TO THE
NATURAL
WORLD

Lifestyles

The reason the Saint of Assisi
Could give his great Song to the Nations
Had much to do with Lifestyle.

Night after night
St. Francis slept in the open
With only the stars as his shelter,
And only the moon as his lamp.

Day after day
He trudged the Umbrian byways,
With fiery sun drenching his body,
And blowing breeze drinking the sweat beads.

Month after month
Francis companioned the waters;
Spring waters that slackened his thirst,
Stream waters that soothed aching feet,
Sacred waters that quickened his soul.

Year after year
St. Francis savored the earth
Which was his bed in the darkness,
Which provided his food through the day —
A continuing resource of power.

Throughout all the span of his living,
Every bird and beast of creation
Was his friend, his sister, his brother,
Part of his family of God.

St. Francis gave us his song
Because it was a vital expression
Of every hour and day of his life.

But what song is singing for us?
From what lifestyles do our lyrics spring?

Our stars are blinded by street lights,
Our sun is hidden by smog.

Air conditioners waft us our breezes,
City zoos provide beasts and birds.

Doctored water comes from steel faucets,
Fruits and foods are frozen or tinned,
And black asphalt encases the earth.

How do we get in touch
With the reality Francis found?
What lifestyles should we be creating?

"Praise Him, All Rivers!"

"Praise the Lord, heaven and earth. Praise Him, all rivers!" That is part of an inscription which Francis had placed above the altar of a tiny chapel which was erected at his direction, long before he wrote "Canticle of the Sun." (p. 221-222 *St. Francis Nature Mystic*, by Edward A. Armstrong, publ. by U. of Cal. Press, 1973)

"Praise Him, all rivers!" What a concept. Francis knew about rivers, intellectually, emotionally, spiritually, and perhaps even sub-consciously, or prophetically.

From the Bible, he knew of the Euphrates in the land from which Abraham migrated under God's guidance to open up new worlds in the history of religious living. And the Nile, homeland of the Egyptians, from which Moses led the children of Israel toward the promised land.

Francis of Assisi had journeyed to the Holy Land and of course had knowledge of the River Jordan where Christ had been baptized. He knew of the Tiber which flowed through the plains near Assisi before becoming the great River of Rome.

He knew of the Arno, whose source was near the Mount of La Verna, where he received the stigmata.

But there were other rivers, Rivers of the Spirit, about which Francis may have been thinking as he caused that inscription to be placed above the altar of the little chapel.

"There is a river, the streams whereof shall make glad the city of God . . ."

Psalm 46:4 (KJV)

St. Francis River near its source in Missouri Ozarks.

". . . and a man shall be as . . . rivers of water in a dry place . . ."

Isa. 32:2 (KJV)

". . . and he shall be like a tree planted by the rivers of water, that bringeth forth his fruit in his season . . ."

Psalm 1:3 (KJV)

"For thus saith the Lord, Behold, I will extend peace to her like a river . . ."

Isa. 66:12 (KJV)

No one knows what was in St. Francis' thoughts, but to have given such an exalted place above the chapel altar to these waterways of the world, whether physical or spiritual, indicated that his mind was groping, his spirit searching. Perhaps even his sub-conscious was feeding his thoughts; whether he sensed it or not, he was raising a curtain on the future.

"Praise Him, all rivers!" Today in America a waterway does just that — the St. Francis River which rises in Missouri's Ozarks and flows across a corner of that state, down through Arkansas, and into the Mississippi below Memphis, Tennessee. On the St. Francis River, State Parks give special attention to preserving God's wild life, National Forests protect the environment, wildlife refuges seek to provide shelter for migrating birds.

The first European to sight the great falls of the Niagara River was a Franciscan. There is the Colorado River whose Grand Canyon was explored by the early Franciscans.

Franciscans journeyed on crude rafts past the mouth of the Mississippi twenty-six years after Columbus' last voyage to the New World and long before the river was discovered by De Soto. Other Franciscans later journeyed along it, as they explored America's heartland.

The Sacramento River, in California, was named by Franciscan fathers for the blessed sacraments so dearly loved by St. Francis.

The Los Angeles River, which gave its name to the city, was in turn named after "Our Lady, Queen of the Angels of Porciuncula," the chapel near Assisi which was the very home of St. Francis' movement.

With prophetic foresight, Francis honored all rivers above his sacred altar.

Sunflowers and Sunlight

If Francis of Assisi had been a modern song writer,
Like Johnny Cash or Bob Dylan,
He wouldn't have been a "Moonlight and Roses" poet.
The "Canticle" was the theme of **his** writing.
He dealt in shafts of strong sunlight,
   Penetrating,
      Purifying,
         Searching,
Filled with fire, yet life-giving,
With healing and warmth in their rays.

And Roses?
Not the hot house varieties, probably.
But wild roses,
Which spring up unsung and unplanted
To give cheer and color
To fence-corners of forgotten fields,
And to obscure crannies of forgotten lives.

Francis of Assisi, if singing today,
Would have been a dandelion and goldenrod poet,
Heralding the lowly blooms
That spread carpets of gold
Over vacant lots and vacant lives
That are suffering from drought and neglect.

He would have been a writer of songs about sunflowers
That light up every lane and field-path and roadway.
His would have been verses
Redeeming the commonplace,
Bestowing Holy Orders on the ordinary.
He was — and would have been today —
A songwriter and poet of living,
Singing of sunflowers and sunlight —
Common things that keep our world bright.

Folklore or Fact?

To many who casually read the story of St. Francis' taming of the wolf of Gubbio, this is smilingly accepted as an innocent legend; his Sermon to the Birds is viewed as a bit of quaint folklore. These are literary excesses, such readers feel, which inevitably build up around great heroes and heroines of history.

True believers in St. Francis take such episodes on faith. Nonbelievers smile — and dismiss them. But there is still another way to approach these strange stories of St. Francis and the natural world. It is a way embedded in the relationship between a God of love and His natural creations. A personal experience serves as an illuminating illustration.

As a means of exercise and as a way of greeting the dawn, I — Francis Line — have for nearly a decade jogged every day of the year, at home or abroad, wherever I may be. In strange cities, strange neighborhoods, such jogging often attracts dogs — sometimes barking dogs, occasionally even dogs that nip at my heels. I have little fear of these animals and do not let them upset me. But once, near my own home, on my own street, a dog — a newcomer to the neighborhood — started barking at my heels each time I passed his domain. I was not deterred, but I did not like it. This went on for a week and even the animal's owner could not stop his forays.

One day our ten year old granddaughter Krista visited us and accompanied me on my morning jog. The barking dog appeared — and approached. "Oh, look," said Krista elatedly. Reaching down, she gave the dog a huge hug. Wagging its tail, the animal jogged along beside us — in silence. It never barked at me again.

I do not FEAR dogs; our granddaughter LOVES them. She reacted to them actively, with the type of love that is God-inspired. There is a world of difference. It is a poor practice for persons in general to hug strange barking dogs. But this incident demonstrated to me the power which God's creative love, shown through a person, can have over an animal.

Another illustration. As makers of documentary educational motion pictures, Helen and I occasionally film animals, and have many friends who are professional wildlife photographers.

Our friends the Crislers, Lois and Herb, were once on assignment for Walt Disney to make a film on Canadian wolves. Before their work was over — so lovingly did they react to these wild creatures — some of the wolves came in and out of their tent at will, without thought of fear from the Crislers. Lois and Herb even learned to understand the "wolf talk" of Lady and Trigger.

Once when Lois was alone with Trigger he growled warningly but she said, "Summoning all the love I really felt for this animal, I kept my hand on his fur. I felt a tuning of love with him as strong and definite as a harp chord strummed. I sensed him as a wild free being, neither doglike nor humanlike, but wolf and wild. His eyes glanced across mine. His defensive growling ceased. From this moment on he was less defensive with me.

"But what on earth had happened? Just this: the wolf had read my eyes! The thing happens so fleetingly, the animal's wild inexorable intelligence seizes the knowledge so instantaneously that the wonder is I ever blundered into awareness of this deepest range of communication. It is, I think, the inner citadel of communication: your true feeling looks out of your eyes, the wild animal reads it." *

In two different homes where we have lived we have entertained families of skunks. Sometimes — completely wild and untreated — they would wander in and out of our house. One of these little wild creatures made its home in our film editing room for a couple of days, as we continued to work there. We had no fear of the skunks, nor they of us. We enjoyed them greatly. In a sense, we loved them.

Love is in the essence of God, and when it replaces fear completely, seeming miracles often occur. Francis of Assisi reflected such love as few others have ever done. He loved birds and beasts actively, creatively, totally. It was perhaps no miracle at all that birds and beasts responded to him as they did, but just a normal reaction to God's love which they felt in his presence. This same quality, bestowed on people, created other so-called miracles. Much of St. Francis' life was a living miracle, because of love.

*From "Arctic Wild" by Lois Crisler. (Pgs. 157-58). Published by Harper & Brothers in 1958. Copyright ©1958 by Lois Crisler, ©1956 The Curtis Publishing Company.

ORCHESTRATIONS
AND
MEDLEY

HIGH – LOW
MUTED – RESONANT
NOTES IN
ST. FRANCIS' LIFE

Where Your Treasure Is —

"Love of money is the root of all evil."
Francis emphasized that concept at times,
But he considered it constantly.
Hand-in-hand with his positive practice of love,
And affirmative concepts of service,
This abhorrence of the worship of money
Was an ingredient of his lifestyle
And global message to people.

He knew that pursuit of money hardens,
Adoration of money debases,
Hoarding of money shrivels
The living soul.

A pack rat gathered treasure and trash in its nest in the authors' back yard.

Not money alone —
But the flood of trinkets and trivia,
The excesses of treasure and trash,
Which it commands,
That weigh one down,
Impede one's life,
Destroy one's values,
And shut one off from God.

The natural gifts of creation,
The friendship and love of his neighbors,
The abundant fruits of the Spirit,
These were the treasures of Francis;
These were the things that he blessed.

Not impediments to living,
Not concoctions of men,
Not crutches for limping.

But stairways to joy,
Ladders toward heaven,
Pathways to contentment,
Passports of the Spirit.

Not love of money,
But of God,
And of God's creations.

Thirteenth Century Protest

St. Francis was a Protestant.
Not ecclesiastically,
Such as Lutheran
Or Methodist
Or member of the Church of Christ.
Protestant denominations
Had not even been heard of then.
Obviously, Francis was a devout Catholic.

Yet, all the same,
Francis of Assisi was a Protestant;
He simply accented the second syllable,
Rather than the first.

Francis was a Pro-**test**-ant.
He questioned the face values about him,
Took not even the sacred for granted,
Refused to worship the god, Status Quo.

Francis tested life by its living,
Used Jesus' scale of values to weigh it,
Then **protested** all that was dross.

He protested the conformity and norm
    of smugness and pride,
    of hatred and greed,
    of violence and conniving.

In their place he set an example
    of caring,
    forgiveness,
    and love.

He protested man's domination
    of Mother Earth,
His disregard for her creatures,
Man's contempt for wildness and nature.

Man and Earth, people and creatures,
Are sisters and brothers, he said.
No longer should they hold the positions
Of Master and slave.

He protested wealth for wealth's sake;
The glitter and gloss of mere show.
He protested religion that's sterile,
Mere piousness without any heart.

Wherever he went St. Francis protested the false,
But in every breath of his life
He protected and worshipped the true.

Francis of Assisi was a Protestant
Who put the emphasis where it counted,
And in so doing
He changed the world.
His emphasis is something to ponder.

A Blessing by St. Francis

"The Lord bless thee, and keep thee:
The Lord make his face shine upon thee,
    and be gracious unto thee:
The Lord lift up his countenance upon thee,
    and give thee peace."

                              Numbers 6:24-26

When one of the closest of his followers, Brother Leo, was severely tempted with discouragement, St. Francis took a parchment on which he had recently composed his great "PRAISE TO THE MOST HIGH GOD," and on its back wrote for his distraught brother the beautiful Biblical blessing from Numbers.

On Brother Leo it had penetrating effect as it had on many before him.

Since Leo's time, the importance of this Bible blessing has been intensified because of its use by St. Francis.

Detail of St. Francis statue, Palm Desert, California.

New Furrows

Francis of Assisi plowed new furrows,
not shallow, as with a wooden plow,
but deep, as with steel.

Fallow ground, long dormant,
was stirred,
received air and sun
to nourish the seeds of change.

The soul of humanity awakened to new concepts
   of love,
   of commitment,
Tasted the new wine
   of the spirit
and accepted the challenge of a life
   of simplicity,
   and service
with gifts of the spirit:

   Love
   Patience
   Joy
   Quietness
   Gentleness
   Peace

   To enfold
   the world.

Reverence for Life

Out of the whirlwind
And fire of war
A youth stepped forth
With a new identity.
He knew who he really was!
His name was Francis of Assisi.

He had fought in the Perugian wars,
And become a prisoner of conflict,
Like a score of other Assisi youth.
In prison he had recognized
His companions with a refreshing
Kind of compassion.
He sensed their needs,
Treating enemies and friends alike.
With dignity and love he encouraged them
To sing of life and of home.
He felt each man was his brother!

When he at last left the prison,
As the iron gates were closing behind him,
He stooped to the earth
And caressed it.
Taking a handful of moist, fragrant soil,
He sensed an intimation of a new song for the world.

Be Praised, O Mother Earth,
My brothers and I, who have suffered
And been denied your fruits,
Will restore you and reverence you.
And you will sustain us!

Francis Bernardone went out to revere and
serve the earth, its creatures, and God.

Out of prison gates, singing as he went,
stepped a youth who would change the world.

The Way-Show-er

Francis of Assisi knew the deep inner secrets of living.

People of his time — thousands of them — had a sense of despair, of gnawing need; their lives were desolate. On such as these, Francis bestowed new life.

For men of wealth, he demonstrated ways of living in which meaning replaced materialism.

To persons of royal blood — even kings and princes — he offered the nobler royalty of inner riches.

He showed soldiers of fortune how the spirit can replace the sword.

He taught tired, pinched personalities on every level of society how to free themselves from slavish conformity and give themselves to a saving Christ.

Not wealth but wisdom. Not pride but humility. Not worldliness but simplicity. Not empty living but heartfilled joy. Not a rock but a loaf. And spiritual water for drink.

People by the thousands followed Francis because he taught them — and by his example he showed them — how to come alive. Then, his mission accomplished, he demonstrated how to die — in dignity and joy.

Untold numbers of people, today as in Francis' time, lead empty lives, bleak existences filled with desolation and despair. Materialism enslaves them; the pace of life overwhelms them. They are suffocated by fears, fads, phobias. They have lost their way in life, and their will to live. But when death approaches, they fear that too, and it looms as their final defeat.

Francis of Assisi knew the deep secrets of living — and of dying. His life, and his death, have infinite lessons for all. He is a way-show-er for those in need.

LOVE SONGS

CLARE AND FRANCIS
LOVE OF GOD
LOVE OF NEIGHBOR
LOVE OF LIFE

Song of Love

The whole world pays homage to a man with a song.
A singing troubadour, with a love song, draws crowds in any age.
Francis was a man with a song on his lips,
But more importantly he had a song in his heart.
      He was irrestible!

Men flocked to his side;
The poor, who were captivated by his joyful singing,
The rich because he offered them the song free.

A lone woman — Clare of Assisi — also caught the rhythm of his
life.
His song and love of Christ filled her being and her thought.
She left family and riches behind,
Allowing Francis' song to fill her whole existence.

That is the REAL story of the love between these two.
Francis and Clare were singing the same lyrics,
A tenor and a soprano,
Blending their melody into perfect harmony.

Their theme song was service to others,
Because Christ's love so filled their hearts.

Francis and Clare both attracted thousands with Christ's theme:
"If I be lifted up I will draw all persons unto me."
Their lives were spent making the song of their LORD come true!
      It became contagious!

In life they comforted each other.
Sublimating their love,
They showed others how to live with courage.
Theirs is a timeless love story; influencing the whole of society.
They made it wholesome by their lives and their love.

      IT IS A SONG TO BE REPEATED FOREVER

The lives of Clare and Francis revolved around the church of San Damiano. It was here that Francis prepared a small convent, where Clare spent much of her life, as head of the Order of Poor Clares. Here St. Clare died. Here St. Francis first sang his Canticle of the Sun. It was here, also, earlier in his life, that Francis, while kneeling before a painting of the crucifix, received the message to rebuild the church. With his own hand labor, he rebuilt the crumbling walls of San Damiano.

Liberated Leader

Women's Liberation;
Much talk of it —
And need for it —
Abound all about us today.

This has been always so.

In Bible times,
Women were sometimes chattels —
Second class citizens at best.
But Jesus came along
And said "No."

He exalted Mary and Martha;
To the woman at the well he gave status;
To Mary Magdalene he made his first resurrection appearance.

So it was with St. Francis.

His second far-flung Order
He placed in charge of a woman.
Clare of Assisi was head and co-founder
Of the Sisterhood of Poor Clares,
Which has gone on to circle the globe.

"St. Clare," "Santa Clara,"
Her name is everywhere.
On cities and institutions of learning;
On lakes, and rivers, and landmarks.

And her influence continues forever,
Spreading leaven and good in the Nations,
All because Francis of Assisi
Understood the potentials of women.

Loving Makes the Difference

What made Francis a Saint?
It was simple,
It was love of God,
And love of neighbor —
That was all.
He was just living Jesus' two Great Commandments.

The only difference —
  He **really** loved.

He loved God
  With all his heart,
  With all his mind,
  With all his soul,
  With all his strength.

And as for his neighbors —
He gave his whole life to them
In loving word
  And deed
  And service.

It is simple, being a saint.
There are just two rules;
  Love God,
  And love your neighbor.

It is simple —
But it isn't easy.

The Secular Order

The spirit of Francis of Assisi's Secular Order was reflected in an open letter which he addressed to all Christians. Even today his words call us:

Love God
Love our neighbors as ourselves
Have charity and humility
Abstain from vice and sin
Keep from excesses in food and drink
Respect the clergy
Do good to those who hate us
Be simple, humble, and pure *

Men, women and families, by the thousands, affiliated themselves with this Secular Order. Reinforced by the spirit and life of St. Francis, they were in reality actually renewing their allegiance to the teaching and spirit of Christ.

*Adapted from "Rebuild My Church," by Luke M. Ciampi O.F.M. (p. 7). Published 1972 by Franciscan Herald Press.

Farm family in fields below Assisi.

"How Beautiful Is a Seed —
O, God, How Beautiful!"

— Francis of Assisi

A seed isn't beautiful — really.
Usually small, dusty brown, odd shaped.
If you didn't know what a seed was
You'd scarcely give it second glance.

It isn't the seed you see,
It's the seed's **becoming**.
It's what's inside,
What's yet to be.

You don't see a wrinkled peach pit,
You see a fine flowering tree and fruit.
You don't see the seed — you see growth.
You see the potential
Within and beyond the shell.

That's the way Jesus looked at people.
Most of them weren't much, really.
Zacchaeus was small.
The prostitute was stained,
Simon was crass.
But Jesus saw within them
What was yet to be.

In Zacchaeus Jesus saw perfection.
In Simon he saw Peter, the Rock.
In the prostitute he beheld a saint.
He saw these people's potentials;
He visioned them into splendor,
Through love.

Francis of Assisi looked at a seed
The way that Jesus looked at people —
Both saw the splendor.

O, GOD, HOW BEAUTIFUL!

A Love Song

O Francis — of Assisi
Your song is one song — we should sing —
It's an Earth Song, a Sun and Moon Song,
Star and Wind and Fire Song — of purest melody.

Chorus

For it's a love song —
A God song —
Love of man song —
Love of bird and beast song —
Full of harmony, don't you see?

It's a song of Sun, our Brother —
And of precious Earth, our Mother —
It's a song of varied weather,
That will bind us all together — in friendly love.

Chorus

It's a song of — praise and glory,
A song to teach earth's story —
So sing it and mean it,
And teach it to our children — everywhere.

Chorus

INTONATIONS
OF
CHRIST

Old Italian statue of St. Francis.

Reflections

"Francis of Assisi was a mirror of Christ."
— *G. K. Chesterton*

Francis of Assisi was poor,
Frail in purse and body.
Slight in physique,
No surplus muscles or strength.
Meager possessions,
Plain sandals, rude cloak, rough cowl.
Not much to look at, really.

But no one ever saw **him** when they looked.
They saw the one he reflected.
He was a **Mirror Of Christ**.

P.S.   When people look at me —
I wonder what they see?

"Follow Me"

"Follow me,' Jesus said.
In times of discouragement
He must have questioned,
"But will they?"

Twelve hundred years came
and went.

A young man of Assisi,
a prisoner of war,

43

Caught a vision of what
   "Follow me" might really
   mean.

That young man began
   following
In the footsteps of his Lord.

Following
   in poverty,
   sacrifice,
   service,
   joy,
   even pain.

Until the marks of the Cross
Seared not only his heart and
      life,
But his hands and feet
and his side.

For twelve hundred years
There had been no follower
Like Francis Bernardone of Assisi.

Francis also called for followers,
Then he, too — in pain and weariness, yet in joy —
Lay down his life.

His call was answered.
Followers came.
First one, then twelve,
Then hundreds, and eventually thousands.

It's been two millennia since Jesus hung on the cross,
And nearly half that time
Since Francis called for followers,
Blessed Sister Death, and expired.
Two men — much alike —
Each with a Life,
And a two-word message
That carries on forever —

"FOLLOW ME."

Booster Stations

On hilltops and in open spaces, microwave boosters pick up original electronic signals, amplify them, and send them on their way, renewed and strengthened so that they eventually span the continent.

Francis of Assisi, nearly 800 years ago, was such a booster or amplifier of Jesus' teachings and spirit and message. St. Francis caught the Christian message clearly in the fine-tuned spiritual antenna of his heart. He absorbed it, lived with it, and sent it with renewed strength across the hills and mountains of the future.

Because of St. Francis and others like him, Jesus' original words reach us with strength and clarity. Now it becomes our turn to be boosters, amplifiers, transmitters.

We can help keep Jesus' message strong and clear and alive.

Happy children at play, Assisi.

45

A Conversation with the Christ Within

You say, Christ, that Francis **ran**
to do your bidding — is that true, Lord?
Was he running a race, Lord?
Who was he competing with?
No one, Lord?
You say that he was in a race with himself — to do God's will?

"YES, FRIEND, THAT WAS ONE OF THE MARKS OF HIS
   DISCIPLESHIP."

You say he went running and singing?
Lord, I want to be a disciple —
But I'm afraid I'm not a runner —
And I can't carry a tune.
You say I don't have to compete with Francis —
Just be myself?

Can I dance?
Now, Lord, that's asking too much!
You say Francis did!
He danced his way through life?
Why, that's impossible!
How could he run and sing and dance
All at the same time?

You say singing and dancing
were also marks of his discipleship?

"Yes, Friend, they were the outward signs of his maturity,
   his love of life, and his joy in me — and his total
   obedience to me!"

Lord, I guess I had a different conception
of what it is to be a disciple!

Imitation of Christ

The stigmata has been called one of the great mysteries of religious history. How could the marks of Christ's wounds on his hands, feet, and side actually appear, twelve hundred years later, on the body of Francis of Assisi?

Intensity is the key.

Francis loved Jesus so intensely — had such empathy for his sufferings, such oneness for his life, such veneration for his words — that Francis entered, heart and soul, into the life of Jesus.

Jesus gave healing to the blind and to the lame;
Francis gave a kiss of love to the leper.

Jesus cautioned against the threats of wealth;
Francis wedded his life to Lady Poverty.

Jesus fasted for 40 days in the wilderness;
Francis, likewise, completed a 40-day fast.

Jesus was the prince of peace;
Peace became a cornerstone of Francis' life.

Jesus said: "Be like little children."
The secret of Francis of Assisi's spiritual genius was
that he retained a childlike wonder throughout his life.

Jesus suffered throbbing pain on the cross;
Francis so identified with Jesus that in thinking about
the crucifixion he endured torturing pain.

Jesus' hands and feet were pierced by nails;
Francis received the stigmata.

Francis' life merged and blended into that of Jesus. The intensity of his love of Christ was greater than had ever been before displayed.

Intensity is the key!

The Christ Design

JESUS CHRIST IS THE KING OF GIVERS!
He gives us inner joy —
He said: "Ask . . . that your joy may be full."

(John 16:24 KJV)

He promises us peace —
Saying: "My peace I give unto you."

(John 14:27 KJV)

Francis of Assisi, in the 13th century,
Chose this Jesus to be his model,
And he used every talent he had
To implement THE CHRIST DESIGN.

He became a Troubadour of joy!
He used his singing and his song to transform people.
He lived "at peace" with those about him.
He erased walls that divide rich and poor.
Love sprang alive in his being.
He expressed in dramatic, poetic form, his inner feelings —
Even the birds and beasts responded to his inner glow.

His life imprinted a new design on his world.

Dare we do this, in the 20th century?
Do we believe it possible
That Christ lives and moves in us,
Enough to transform our world?

Is the Christ Design alive in us?

INSTRUMENT
OF THY
PEACE

The Spark of Christ Within

Wonder what Francis of Assisi would say and think if he came to
Our Town today?

Possessions — what a saturation of them we have which
get in the way of true living.
Over-eating — how we stuff and gorge while our
neighbors go hungry — or starve.
Over-drinking — drugging our brains until we lose
control of our bodies, our actions, our cars —
spewing death and destruction along the routes we travel.

Television — dancing colored pictures hallucinating an
entire population — two hundred million of us in a single
evening —
Glued to froth from a glowing tube that commandeers our
existence.

Noise — pollution — commercials —
Saturday night Specials — H Bombs — munitions —
Headlines — trivia — gossip —
Beer halls — porno — lust.

Francis of Assisi would look at it all — comprehend the
meanings — and whisper:

Where there is hatred — let me put love
Where there is anger — let me put forgiveness
Where there is discord — let me bring harmony
Where there is sadness — let me bring joy
Where there is darkness — let me bring light.

Francis of Assisi would look at our world and realize
that this is not the way we really want to live.

Freed of our hatreds, our anger, our sadness,
our lives would begin to shine.

Freed of our discords, our world would begin to
change.

Freed of our darkness, we would become
children of light,
and begin to live
the way that God intended.

Francis of Assisi would look past the shadows —
Past the insecurities, the hatreds, the lust,
To the spark of Christ within,
To the reality of God in us all,
Waiting to be set aflame.

Then through word and deed,
Through love and caring,
Through dedication and service,
Through the saving grace of Christ himself,
He would help to ignite the spark in us all,

So we could start living again!

The Prayer of St. Francis

Lord, make me an instrument of Thy peace;
Where there is hatred let me put love,
Where there is anger let me put forgiveness,
Where there is discord let me put unity,
Where there is doubt let me put faith,
Where there is error let me put truth,
Where there is despair let me bring happiness,
Where there is sadness let me bring joy,
Where there is darkness let me bring light.

O Master grant that I may desire rather:
To console than to be consoled,
To understand rather than to be understood,
To love rather than to be loved.

Because it is in giving that we receive;
In forgiving that we obtain forgiveness;
In dying that we rise to eternal life.

Harmonics

"Make me an instrument of Thy peace," prayed Francis.
Not **You,** but **Me,** were his words.
Not **My** peace, but **Thine,** he said.
Not a **Tool** — such as knife, or gouge, or hatchet,
      hammer, ramrod, or flail.
But an **Instrument** — a conveyor of harmonies —
      a violin, a flute, or bell harp,
      harmonica, harpsichord, lute,
      Carrying accord in its very essence;
      Peace with each chord of its score.

"Make me an instrument of Thy peace," prayed Francis.

Stringed Harmonies (The authors' granddaughter).

53

Testing the Prayer of St. Francis

Francis of Assisi's great prayer instructs us to replace
    hatred with love,
    anger with forgiveness,
    trouble with joy,
    discord with harmony,
    darkness with light.

In producing a documentary motion picture on St. Francis, for use in public schools, we intended to use and illustrate those words, provided they were valid.

But how to know? Are they even possible? Are such options practical in our rough-hewn 9 to 5 business encounters? Were these just cloistered phrases, we wondered, or could they be relied on as living rules for people who work, sweat, and bleed when scratched?

"Let's put them to a test," one of us suggested; and for two months, every day, we started out with that prayer in our minds, seriously trying to adhere to its directives.

On the second day of the test, in a cafe parking lot, a man in a large Cadillac scraped the rear bumper of our Volkswagen, laying open a cruel gouge in the side of his car, but not even scratching ours.

He was clearly at fault but, jumping out of his car, he fumed at my husband as the two of them inspected the damage.

"Damn; look at that." The Cadillac driver's face was reddening and his voice was rising. "That's at least three or four hundred dollars to fix." His glare switched from the car damage to my husband.

We had repeated that prayer — two or three times — not over an hour before, and I wondered under these trying circumstances if its directive would be remembered by my husband. Its phrases were floating still undigested somewhere inside of me along with the eggs and toast.

In a quietness of voice and manner which was quite a marvel to hear, my husband explained that he had stopped, had honked,

54

had even double-honked and shouted as the crash became certain.

"Where there is discord, let me put harmony."

The St. Francis prayer tells what to do initially, but leaves one unprepared for results. Our adversary reddened deeper, swore harder, then suddenly slumped over with what proved to be a mild heart attack.

We summoned help. Responding to the emergency in every way we could we helped him into his car and did everything possible to render aid. When at last the crisis was over the man reached out his hand. He said: "That accident was completely my fault. I want to thank you for everything. My heart attack might have been a lot worse if you'd gotten mad too. You've revealed the most generous spirit of anyone I've ever met."

As we drove home, thanking God, both of us realized that it had been the spirit of St. Francis' prayer that had been revealed. We still try to let its spirit guide our lives and we meditate on its content every day.

— Helen Line

Legendary Saint

Some of the most inspired of the Psalms of David
Are said to have been written
   by others.

Similarly, there are those who determine
That St. Francis' greatest Prayer of Compassion
Was penned by some anonymous admirer.

"Make me an instrument of Thy Peace."
That, truly, is in the spirit of Francis.

If he did not write it
He clearly inspired it.
If its words did not flow from his pen
Assuredly they flowed from his life.

Also, certain of the LEGENDS regarding this Saint
Are thought to be simply that — only legends.
If they are forgeries, which sprang up after his death,
It is because Francis, in life,
Forged on the anvil of anguish
The truths that have made them immortal.

The prayer — the legends —
They are all most certainly of —
If not all actually by —
The humble Saint of Assisi.

GRACE NOTES

MINOR CHORDS
FROM A RETREAT
WITH ST. FRANCIS

A Retreat with St. Francis and His Song

"Canticle of the Sun," with its praises for all of God's creatures, is such a vital expression of life that we decided to make a special Silent Retreat to study and absorb some of its more subtle meanings.

The spirit of the Canticle began to penetrate our thinking and the spirit within us said "Keep it short, like a Haiku."

Francis' great song came alive for us as we gave our own expressions, in lean wordage, to some of its concepts. On the pages which follow are short crystallized thoughts that emerged from that close contact with the Canticle.

Good Relations

God's his Father,
Earth's his Mother,
The Moon's his Sister,
And Wind's his Brother.
For a man who never married,
St. Francis had quite a family.

Study War No More

Brother, Sister, Mother,
All the earth is kin.
Time for wars is over.
Let Brotherhood begin.

Time out for checkers.

Sainted Symbols

All life was symbolic, in Francis' eye;
Earth and water, clouds and sky.

The warming sun was a smile of God;
Love was a path, that Christ had trod.

He saw God's Light in Brother Fire;
The singing larks were a Holy choir.

Wind was God's breath that cools the world;
Blowing grasses were banners of God unfurled.

The Crib was the symbol for sacred birth;
God's symbol for bounty was Mother Earth.

There were signs of God in a young doe leaping;
The rain was God's tears of joyous weeping.

Pain and suff'ring were not appalling;
They were simply symbols of Heaven calling.

Death was God's message of final glory;
For Francis, all Life was a sacred story.

Brother Rock

Humility's not a virtue
With which we humans treat each other.
One must be truly humble
To call a rock "My Brother."

Earth Born

Every day Francis saw the earth as being born
In the splendor and glory of
Brother Sun!

Daily Dozen

"Be Praised, Most High."
That's a good phrase to memorize
And repeat a dozen times each day.

Gift Wrapped

Francis praised all weather; with him we say:
"Fog is God's way
Of wrapping us
In His stillness."

Pioneers

Dante, Columbus, Junipero Serra —
They all wore Franciscan robes,
And penetrated new frontiers!

Weather Or No

"Everyone talks about the weather,"
So the saying goes,
"But no one ever does anything about it."
St. Francis did —
He Enjoyed It.
And he said:
"All weather is good —
But in different ways."

Awake

Praise and
Thanksgiving
filled
Francis'
heart
as he watched
birds and
small creatures
emerge from
night's sleep.
The birds
came out
singing
the dawn
awake!

The Birds

Francis loved to see the birds
in flight
Embroidering the sky
With wind notes.

Detail of St. Francis statue, St. Margaret's Episcopal Church, Palm Desert, California.

Love

Few people remember the splendidly-robed
Popes of Rome, in St. Francis' time,
Who uttered pious pronouncements to the throngs,
    But few can forget the poorly clad
    Joy-filled man of Assisi,
Who preached sermons of love to the birds.

God Knows

St. Francis blessed his friends the birds,
    Then spoke for them a sermon.
Did his message reach his feathered friends?
    That's for God to determine.

The Sun

The morning sun
A luminous light,
Guided Francis' steps aright.

The Water

Humble water fills the wash tub,
Pure water quenches thirst,
Useful water turns the mill wheel,
Sacred water christens birth.

Serenade

Francis listened
To the birds sing —
And called them God's little
Orchestra of joy!

Words To Ponder

"Praise, Glory, Honor"
With those words
Francis commenced his great song.

Those are the ways, also,
With which he began
Each day of his life.

Bless The Beasts

"God's Creatures" was the title
Francis gave to beasts and birds.
He made all life our brothers,
With those immortal words.

Reflection

The pool of water seemed alive —
As St. Francis drank he kissed her —
She reflected back his greeting —
Francis called her "Sister."

Rain Drops

Francis called all weather good
    And praised it in God's sight.
He even blessed the rain drops
    Which soaked his forest bed at night.

Four Letter Words

Francis didn't shun four-letter words
They were the theme and substance of his song
Wind   Fire   Moon   Star   Love
        Most   High.

Toying Around

St. Francis — despite his following —
    Is far from being
The most popular saint in America.
Santa Claus still holds the record.

Refreshing water. Beaver statue in Switzerland.

Rain

Rain waters the earth,
Replenishes rivers —
It gives drink to the creatures,
And nourishment to all that grows.

Rain cleanses the world;
Be praised for Brother Rain!

Our Mother, the Earth
And our Father, the Sky
Are in harmony —
And as it rains we know —
Earth and Sky are making love.

Out of this conception
Spring will emerge —
A tender, beautiful child!

Our Sister, Mother Earth, is singing:
"Rain, our Brother Rain,
Is refreshing our Spirits again."

EXERCISES
AND
ETUDES

KEEPING IN TUNE

Keeping in Tune

Francis of Assisi's Song of the Creatures,
A Canticle of the Sun,
Can be read, in a spirit of quietness, as a poem,
Prayed, in a spirit of worship, as a prayer,
Or experienced, as a set of sacred exercises,
To clarify, sanctify, and re-awaken
All aspects of life.

The reading as poetry takes a moment,
Its use as a prayer may fill an hour.
To experience it as a sacred exercise
May take, at the least, a day, a week, or a month,
And eventually extend through the entire span
of one's life.

Let us analyze the exercise now —
Start to explore the depths of Francis' song.
Then we can spend the rest of our lives in its singing.

Be praised, my Lord, of all your creature world,
And first of all Sir Brother Sun,
Who brings the day, and light you give to us through him,
And beautiful is he, agleam with mighty splendor:
Of you, Most High, he gives us indication.

There begins **Exercise One.**

It cannot be done in a house, or anywhere inside.
It can be accomplished only under a cloudless sky.
To do this exercise we must — in certain seasons — sometimes
wait for days. But with the waiting, comes reward.

At last the day arrives.
The sun in all its blazing power
Is there in the clear sky above.
We go out to greet it,
Stand in the glow of its warmth
And experience its message.
Our Exercise begins.

Sun that brings us light,
How well you tell of your Creator.
We let your rays touch our closed eyelids,
We feel the shower of those piercing shafts of heat,

Prickly sensations of healing power
Entering and penetrating to every cell of our bodies.
Both symbolically and actually
We are bathing — being showered — in light.

Healing light. Penetrating light.
A spiritual, physical massage of splendor.
We stand, absorbed and absorbing,
Not too long.
The power of the sun is mighty
And only a little is needed.
But we stand until we feel the healing.
We have touched, and been touched,
    By Brother Sun.
And thus brought closer to **You.**

"Be Praised, My Lord,
Through Sisters Moon and Stars."
Those are the ingredients of Exercise Two
For which again we must bide our time.

At last the night arrives.
A Moon. Great Planets.
A sky dusted with distant stars,
Mysterious universes of Your creating.
The moon is the maiden of the night.
Her message is of gentleness, softness, and love.
But the stars — that's where the real stretching comes.
"More in number than the sands," said the Psalmist.
A billion, trillion miles distant, according to the
                              Astronomer's measure,

Yet that light — that shaft of **Your** creation,
Comes across those inscrutable distances — to us.
Eternity is piercing our vision;
Across a billion miles, God is speaking to us.
Mystery, Awe, Wonder.
Your universe, God, sings of **Your** glories;
We have had an exercise in Infinity.

"Be Praised, My Lord,
Through Sister Water,
For greatly useful, lowly, precious, chaste is she."
Our Exercise with water becomes at once
    Refreshing
    Cleansing
    Humbling
    and as sacred as a holy vessel.

Water!
How we must exercise to revere it.
We have wasted it with abandon;
We have polluted it like animals.
    No — not like animals,
    For they respect it far more than do we.
Through insensitivity we have cheapened its wonder.
We have been almost blind to its beauty.

Yet water is the blood of our life.
Only a few days can we sustain life without it.
Without water, food would not grow.
Without water, streams would not flow.
Without seas of water, winds would not blow,
And rain would dry up in the skies.

For every glass of water on our table,
Every tub of water in our bath,
For waterfall, rivers, and oceans,
For each drop of dew on the grasses,
Every bead of sweat on our bodies,
Each flake of snow in the mountains
We should give thanks
And kneel in worship
To You.
Water provides us a vast exercise
In humility, purity, awe.

Grape harvest at Assisi.

Be praised, O Lord, through our sister Mother Earth,
For she sustains and guides our life,
And yields us divers fruits, with tinted flowers, and grass.
Be Praised, Most High,
For **all Your** creatures.''

''Mother Earth,''
Here is an **Exercise** in which we can feel sheer grandeur.
    The sun we can sense,
    The stars we can see,
    But Mother Earth is close at hand to our touch.
        Barefooted, we can feel the earth as we step,
        We can sift earth's soil through our fingers
        And wonder at its being, at the same time,
            both common and precious.
        It is the Mother of all that we eat,
        From its womb, every living thing grows,
            Giant redwood and slender reed,
            Flowers and fruit.

The Earth indeed is our Mother.
Yet we have treated her each day like a harlot.
We scar the earth with great tractors —
Mutilating and mangling her surface,
Then with ribbons of asphalt
We attempt to bind up the wounds.

We strip-mine,
We bulldoze,
We deplete the soil of its substance.
We desecrate earth's gentle landscape
With billboards, sky scrapers, slums.

800 years have passed since Francis told us
That the Earth should govern us,
Rather than that we should try to govern her.

We have pretended that we could be masters,
But now the Earth is rebelling.
The greatest **Exercise** of our century
Will come in learning to respect Mother Earth.

As we do so,
We will learn to respect **You**, Most High,
Learn to worship **You** truly,
As St. Francis said that we should.

Be Praised, Most High, for **all** your creatures,
    Sun, wind, stars,
    Water, fire, Earth.
    Even as **You** have created us.
    So **You** are the Creator and Father of all.

ELEGY

A MELODY
AT PARTING

Forgiveness, Peace, Love

"Father, forgive them, for they know not what they do."

That capsule of love, expressed in agony by Jesus as he hung suspended between life and death on the cross of his executioners, is the ultimate example of a forgiving spirit.

St. Francis, shortly before his own death, added two verses to his original Canticle, the first of which sang of the spirit of forgiveness which his Model had demonstrated. As in the case of Jesus, it was not an abstract preachment, but was directed toward a real, immediate problem, in real, immediate concerns of living.

The bishop and the mayor of Assisi had had a quarrel. Their feelings and their fury festered until the ultimate transpired — excommunication of the mayor by the bishop; ugly economic reprisals against the bishop by the mayor.

Francis, on his deathbed, learned of this desolating fever blister of hatred which was festering in his beloved Assisi.

Forgiveness. Peace. Love.

Broken fences in Assisi.

Would people never learn? Instinctively Francis uttered the words which were to become an immortal verse of his Canticle. These words concerning forgiveness were spoken on his deathbed, but they were a summation of his entire life of devotion and service to his neighbors and to God.

> Be praised, my Lord, through those who pardon
>   give for love of you,
> And bear infirmity and tribulation:
> Blessed they who suffer it in peace,
> For of you, Most High, they shall be crowned.

The new verse of the Canticle reached the ears and the consciences of the quarreling Assisi leaders. Their differences melted away; once more they became friends as a spirit of forgiveness dissolved their dispute.

Forgiveness. Peace. Love.

The words — and the message — of this new verse have reached out to the ears and the lives of millions. To those who have been distraught by anger, possessed by hate, or shriveled by an unforgiving spirit and a lack of love, the words — when heeded — have become a healing balm. The verse which Francis sang on his Assisi deathbed became new words of life for the world.

Markings

Hands, feet, side —
There the wounds were inflicted
As Jesus was nailed to the cross.

Hands, feet, side —
There the wounds made their marks
When St. Francis received the stigmata.

Marks of the cross,
Marks of suffering,
Marks of discipleship,
Marks which imprinted their meaning,
Not on his body alone,
But on the very core of his heart.
And yet through it all he was joyful.

Hands, feet, side —
Can we, too, feel the imprint
Of our own marks as disciples?

Hands which grow wrinkled in service of God,
Feet which grow weary in following God,
Heart and side which are aching, sometimes breaking,
As we share with family and neighbors
Some of the love of God.

Marks of discipleship, all;
Can we experience them also
And still be as joyful as Francis?

The Final Verse

As Francis of Assisi lay dying, he asked Brother Leo and Brother Angelo to sing for him his blessed "Canticle of the Sun."

They did so, but as their voices trailed off, Francis himself continued the refrain. What he was singing, however, was a verse which was unfamiliar to their ears.

Just as the other verses could not have been sung by Francis until he had experienced them in his living — for the Canticle was not a product of intellect but of experiential feeling — so this final verse could not have been added until now. Its theme was death, and he was experiencing death as he sang it:

Be praised, my Lord, through our Brother Death of Body,
From whom no man among the living can escape.
Woe to those who in mortal sins will die;
Blessed those whom he will find in your most holy graces,
For the second death will do no harm to them.
Praise and bless my Lord, and thank him too,
And serve him all, in great humility.

Divine Coincidence

As Francis of Assisi lay dying, he asked that his Brothers disrobe him so that, like his divine Model, he could die unencumbered by the goods of this life. His bare body lay on Mother Earth.

At that moment, a multitude of hooded larks, his favorite birds, circled — singing — overhead.

So the legend goes. It is hard to prove or disprove.

This author can simply relate an authentic incident from his own experience. In the last year of her life my eighty-eight-year-old mother had been deeply interested in the phenomenon of migration, with respect to both animals and birds. She asked that I get her the book, the last — save the Bible — which she read: "BIRD MIGRATION" by Donald Griffin.

We held our Mother's Memorial Service in our own large living room, its five enormous windows overlooking the Pacific Ocean. Our minister and I both gave tributes. As the minister concluded his prayer of Gratitude, out there over the sea just beyond the windows a great flash of gulls appeared, circled toward our home, then slowly, majestically sailed away into the distance.

The flight of the sea gulls and of the hooded larks, I have no doubt, were both natural and normal. But, using the terminology of Archbishop Temple, they were **"Divine Coincidences."**

Hymns of Creation

Francis of Assisi was a Troubadour of Joy, journeying always on an ascending scale of nobility, set to life's rhythm and music.

Music of the running streams,
Joyful songs of the birds,
Especially Sister Lark.
Music in the stars at night,
And the glowing sun at dawn.
Music of blowing wind and dripping fog.

Orchestrations of joy.
Dancing stacattos of raindrops,
Symphonies of solitude.
Great hymns of creation
Sung by all of God's creatures.

Music of love in people,
Peasants working the fields,
Children at play.
Poor people struggling in cities,
Beggars, lepers, outcasts,
Noblemen, Sultans, Popes.
All sacred notes to St. Francis.

Then — mournful bars of suffering,
Quiet pianissimos of pain,
And the final reverent elegy of death.
But even then, music on his lips.

Like the Morning Star

In a sermon which he preached at Assisi at the canonization of St. Francis, just two years following the Franciscan Founder's death, Pope Gregory IX applied to Francis the beautiful descriptive words from Ecclesiasticus (Sirach), found in Catholic editions of the Bible.

"He shone in his days as the morning star in the midst of a cloud, and as the moon at the full.

And as the sun when it shineth, so did he shine in the temple of God.

And as the rainbow giving light in the bright clouds, and as the flower of roses in the days of the spring, and as the lilies that are on the brink of the water, and as the sweet smelling frankincense in the time of summer.

As a bright fire, and frankincense burning in the fire.

As a massy vessel of gold, adorned with every precious stone.

As an olive tree budding forth, and a cypress tree rearing itself on high, when he put on the robe of glory, and was clothed with the perfection of power" (Eccli. 50:6-11).

From "As the Morning Star," by Marion Habig O.F.M., p. 19.

Assisi field worker before Sacro Convento. St. Francis is buried in Basilica below tower in rear.

The Test

To praise Mother Earth as our Sister
Gives no one cause for complaint,
But to bless Sister Death at one's dying,
Is surely the mark of a Saint.

ARIAS
FROM
ASSISI

Assisi — Old and New

On our first visit to Assisi, in 1959, on the plain below the city we came upon an entire family working together in the hayfield, with two fine white oxen pulling the hay cart. As the family ate their simple lunch together at noontime they brought from a well great buckets of cool water for the oxen to drink. The animals gurgled their thanks!

A dozen years later, on another Assisi visit, we found the same man of that family — working alone now — plowing his field. No oxen this time; they had been replaced by a shiny red tractor.

At noon time, after he had eaten his lunch alone, the man poured a can of gasoline into the tractor's fuel tank. When he started the machine it snorted its thanks in a clatter of deafening noise.

> One man replaces the family.
> A tractor replaces the oxen.
> Gasoline replaces cool water.
> Noise and power for thanks.
> **Time Marches On In Assisi.**

Assisi Dawn

We awoke to a golden dawn.
The quiet of beautiful Assisi lay around us,
Transforming everything.
We stood at the window and marvelled
At the light and shadows playing
Across the Umbrian plains below,
With Perugia in the distance, high on its hill.
A city of Ancient Days!

Church bells tolled our spirits awake
And birds carolled their songs to our ears.
The city began to stir.
Francis, of this Italian hillside village,
Once strode through its streets,
And sang his songs,
Preached to the birds,
Became its messenger of gladness!

We felt his spirit filling us
With the wonder of his life,
And we stepped forth
To the wonder of our own!

The glorious golden glow
        of dawn
Trims the whole world
        With halos!

Troubadours of Joy!

The dedicated lovers of St. Francis — on a journey to Assisi — always make a Pilgrimage. They climb the wooded path up Mount Subasio to the Hermitage, where Francis often stayed.

But they don't just walk. They sing as they go, singly, in pairs, small groups, or whole platoons, swinging and singing their way up the mountain. As they go up, they sing in anticipation. Coming down, they sing for pure joy at the spiritual adventure which has been theirs.

They are the modern troubadours of joy!

A City and A Saint

Rome's glory is many-splendored:
Caesars, Popes, Colosseum, St. Peter's, the Forum —
These and more are ingredients of its greatness.

The fame of Paris is such that one despairs
at listing its landmarks;
London so noted that it scarce adds or detracts
That Dickens once lived in its boundaries.

But Bethlehem, known over Christendom,
Is important for one fact alone —
There the Christ child was born.
There the Incarnation was nourished.

And Nazareth forever is chronicled
As locus for the boyhood of Jesus.

It is so with Assisi.
This Italian city of beauty
Is a repository of art and of treasure,
A city of charm and of churches,
With hilltop castles and ruins,
Vineyards in Umbrian landscape below.

But Pilgrims don't come for the castle,
Tourists don't come for the churches,
Franciscans from over the world
Do not seek Assisi
Just for art or for treasure.

They come because a Man —
A breathing soul who altered the Ages
In his manner of worship and action —
Once dwelt in this town of Assisi.

Not the city, but the Saint,
Is the essence of its greatness.

Assisi Treasure

In Assisi we stayed and studied in the "Christian Observatory" — one of the world's most complete storehouses of books, recordings, and art works on the life of Christ. Here we had access to 45,000 photographs of the works of both contemporary and ancient artists concerning his life. There were 2500 authentic prints on this subject.

In the 7th floor music room of this architecturally-splendid building designed by an Italian woman to fit into and blend with the rose-colored stone of old Assisi, and yet to be most modern — were 4000 recordings and items singing Christ's glory. The great library had 35,000 volumes, and more than one million reference cards concerning Christian literature.

We stayed in special quarters where pilgrims from across the world can find accommodations. Here are enormous kitchens and a dining room which seats several hundreds.

The Christian Observatory is part of the Pro Civitate Christiana, a dedicated band of men and women, all university graduates, who do not marry but live and work here, giving their lives in an unselfish way, to assist in the physical and spiritual renewal of Italy. Vows are taken by all, making them almost "modern Franciscans."

But the supreme adventure of our "Observatory" stay was to see the collection of paintings and sculpture in modern, well-lighted galleries extending up floor upon floor — 700 paintings and art works on display.

Many pertained to various aspects of Christ's life. But the collection that is in itself worth a visit to Assisi is the exhibit, "Jesus Divine Worker," showing him as craftsman and builder. Great artists have imaginatively painted him in half a hundred different aspects of building — working with plane and mallet at his carpenter's bench, drilling boards with an auger, erecting the heavy beams of a house, using chisel and hammer, constructing a wheel, working from a ladder, using a plumb line, even physically constructing a church.

These paintings helped us realize more clearly than ever how closely St. Francis had followed his Model. One of the great turning

Flowers spring from the ruins of old Assisi.

points in Francis of Assisi's life occurred when, from the crucifix at the old crumbling church of San Damiano, he heard a voice saying: "Rebuild my church." Francis took the directive literally and devoted himself to intensive manual labor repairing the dilapidated and collapsing walls of San Damiano, and other churches. As Jesus before him, he actually became carpenter and builder.

Later, he took a broader interpretation of the directive which he had received, and worked to renew the spirituality of the whole Church which Christ had established.

The "Jesus Divine Worker" collection in Assisi emphasizes the seldom-mentioned fact that both Jesus and Francis, literally and figuratively, were builders. The visitor to this great collection reads the words of Pope Pius XII: "Do not doubt, for Christ is always with you. Think to see Him where you work."

NEW WORLD SYMPHONY

ST. FRANCIS' INFLUENCE SPREADS TO AMERICA

Columbia!

Nearly everywhere that Francis of Assisi journeyed during his lifetime, he attracted — by his example, his convictions, and the strength and spirituality of his personality — new adherents to his movement. Following his death the movement continued to expand, nourished by a yearning of people for new lifestyles of simplicity and new dimensions of spiritual living.

"Go all over the world with that Song," Francis had told his followers as he finished singing his Canticle of the Sun. The Franciscans did just that, carrying the rhythm of his music, and the spirit of his life with them as they went.

Years passed. Some crossed the Alps into central Europe. Others went to Spain. Still others went to the new world, probably on the second voyage of Columbus, who himself donned the robes of a Franciscan.

St. Francis' influence began spreading across the mysterious continent which would be known as America.

A new world era had begun.

*Columbus statue in Genoa, Italy
faces toward the New World.*

Song In Orbit

As Francis finished singing his praises to nature, he said: "We must go all over the world with that Song, singing like birds!"

This was a challenge;
Just as Jesus had told his disciples:
"Go into all the world and
Preach the Gospel."

Jesus' message to the world was a
Message of Love —
God is our Father,
Making us **One!**
And I leave my Peace with you,
That you may be filled with **Joy!**

Francis' message was in reality the same. He said:
Take That Song All Over the World,
Proclaiming
All men and women are **Kin**
All creatures are **Kin** to us!
All Life Is Sacred,
Go Singing, Like Birds,
So people will stop and listen
And Be Joyful!

Francis and Jesus —
Intertwined — interwoven
Into the Fabric of Life.
Love, Joy, Peace,
Oneness — Wonderfulness —
        Everlasting!

Three Songs in One?

When Francis of Assisi instructed his followers to carry his Song over the world, he was making certain that its words and its message would spread not only to far horizons geographically, but that its very meanings would expand linguistically as it swept into new countries and found expression in different languages.

This is because the small word "per" has multiple meanings in the land where Francis first used it in each verse of his immortal song.

Some English translators have said: "Be praised, Most High, **for** Brother Sun, and **for** Sister Moon, Brother Wind," etc.

Others have translated it: "Be praised, Most High, **by** Brother Sun."

And still others: "Be praised, Most High, **through** Brother Sun." It can even be translated as "with" or "on account of."

There are those who suggest that St. Francis realized as he sang it, that this tiny word was so wide in scope that it could embrace these multiple concepts.

It is an interesting exercise to read the Canticle, using first the word "for," then the word "by," and finally "through." All three meanings are deeply true. Each concept expands the nature of the song and the breadth of its application. God's realm widens with each such reading. In a sense, St. Francis has given us three immortal songs in one.

His Name is on the Land

In 1609, nearly a dozen years in advance of, and 2000 miles westward from the Pilgrim's landing on Plymouth Rock, an obscure follower of St. Francis gave the name to Santa Fe, now New Mexico's capital city. "La Villa de Santa Fe de San Francisco," he called it — "The city of the Holy Faith of St. Francis." That is still its full name.

A lifetime earlier — 1539 — a Franciscan who was scouting the land for the eventual exploration by Coronado raised a flag near what is now the boundary between New Mexico and Arizona, naming that vast area of the southwest the "Kingdom of St. Francis." Today, Arizona's highest mountains — the San Francisco Peaks — rise over that land, commemorating the name of the Assisi Saint.

In 1776, the de Anza expedition journeyed from Mexico to the central California coast for the express purpose of establishing a city to honor the Franciscan founder — San Francisco. The Mission Dolores, which still serves the city, is officially Mission "San Francisco de Asis."

A few miles southward is Mission "Santa Clara de Asis" and the city and county of Santa Clara, commemorating the lovely girl of Assisi whom Francis loved, and with whom he helped found the Second Order of Franciscans — the Poor Clares.

In 1769, the Spanish explorer, Ortega — advance scout for the Portola Expedition — pitched camp near a small Pacific Coast river. The date was August 1, sacred day of the tiny Portiuncula chapel, which had been Francis' headquarters in Assisi. So the spot was named "Nuestra Senora La Reina de Los Angeles de Portiuncula," or Our Lady the Queen of the Angels of Portiuncula. Twelve years later when de Nave founded a city here, it was given this name — later shortened to Los Angeles.

To the north, the Sacramento River was named by the Spaniards for the Sacraments, which were so precious to Francis, and later California's capital city was given the name Sacramento.

The degree of Franciscan influence on California place names is shown by the fact that over 50 of her communities, a quarter of her counties, and more than 300 rivers, peaks, islands, and other geographic features are named after saints or religious objects.

The name of St. Francis is on the land in English, Spanish and French. Mid-America is dotted with places named in his honor. A portion of the Missouri Ozarks is called the St. Francois Mountains. The St. Francis River rises here, flowing through St. Francois County, Missouri, and on past St. Francis, Arkansas.

The name of Francis of Assisi is also on the land in Texas. In the 1680's a cluster of missions was established by the Franciscans near what is now El Paso. In 1690, in what is now East Texas, Franciscans built the first mission in this part of the country. This mission, moved to San Antonio, was originally called **"San Francisco de la Tejas,"** after St. Francis and the Tejas, or Texas Indians.

In San Antonio the Franciscans also founded the Mission San Antonio de Valero. Near by grew some cottonwood trees, which in Spanish are known as **"Alamos."** This became the popular name for this part of the old Mission when in 1836 it became the Cradle of Texas Independence.

Francis of Assisi died more than half a thousand years before America became a nation but across the entire continent, from Florida to the Golden Gate — his name is on the land.

St. Francis of the Guns

Following the assassination of Senator Robert Kennedy in California, the people of San Francisco responded to the public pleas from Mayor Joseph Alioto and voluntarily turned in their guns to police authorities.

Some 2,000 guns were turned in, and from those weapons, melted down, an imposing statue called St. Francis of the Guns was created by sculptor Beniamino Bufano.

The dedication of the statue took place before San Francisco's city hall on June 6, 1969. At the ceremony, people of every nationality, several thousands of them, repeated Francis' great prayer:

"Make Me an instrument of Thy peace;
where there is hatred, let me put love."

After its dedication, the statue was sent on a goodwill journey along California's mission trail, which culminated in San Diego for the celebration of that city's 200th anniversary. St. Francis of the Guns was retracing the route which Father Junipero Serra, inspired by St. Francis, had walked two centuries before.

Later, the statue went to Japan, to carry the Franciscan message of peace and goodwill to the millions who attended that nation's World's Fair. As this St. Francis likeness continues to be seen by people of all the world, its symbolism carries on the message of the Assisi saint.

At dedication of ST. FRANCIS OF THE GUNS statue, San Francisco, California.

Miracle of 32nd Street

Mid-town Manhattan, off Broadway,
Is not the most inspiring place in our land.
Clerks and shop people, spewed from the subways,
Hurry to offices and stores.
Commuters, jolted into Penn Station from Long Island,
Scurry to sanctuary sky scrapers.
Tourists, street-walkers, pan-handlers,
Motley habitants of a brick-encased jungle,
Stream back and forth along 32nd Street's crowded sidewalks
Intent on the tasks of the day,
Or the pleasures of the evening.

But in a tiny court
Not a dozen feet from this traffic,
Nestled behind a church of St. Francis,
Is a kneeling statue of the Assisi Saint.
Some people step into the church,
Others pause a second
And whisper a prayer.
Some touch Francis' hand or knee with their fingers,
Some just hesitate — to look,
And then continue on.

There has been a moment of uplift.
Inspiration has found its way to these sidewalks.
The spirit of a Saint has blessed the multitudes,
And the bronze statue is shiny with gentle touches of love.

A never-ceasing miracle
Is unfolding in the canyons of mid-Manhattan
Because Francis of Assisi is there.

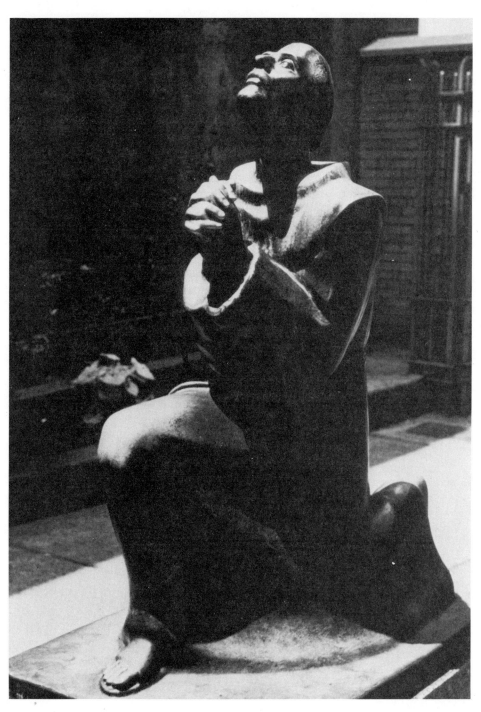

Statue of St. Francis, St. Francis Church, mid-Manhattan, New York.

Tree of Life

In the United States Capitol Building in Washington, D.C. stands a statue of one of America's most beloved Franciscans, Junipero Serra, founder of the California Missions which extend from San Diego in the south to Mission San Francisco de Solano at Sonoma in the north. Among them are "San Francisco de Asis," in San Francisco, and "Santa Clara de Asis" in nearby Santa Clara.

"Junipero" was not Father Serra's given name. Born on the Island of Majorca in the Mediterranean Sea off Spain, he was christened "Miguel Jose." But he so loved and admired Brother Juniper, one of St. Francis' original followers, that he voluntarily chose it to be his name.

The story is told that when Francis of Assisi met the man who was to become Brother Juniper, and learned his name, he said: "So please it God that upon your branches thousands of souls shall build their nests!" (Kazantzakis)

Junipero Serra was one of those souls, and Serra's influence in early California carried on the spirit and influence and love of Brother Juniper, and of St. Francis. Like the seeds of a Juniper tree spread by the birds, wild animals, and the wind, that influence continues, never ending.

SONG OF THE EARTH

A PATRON SAINT FOR ECOLOGISTS

Quality vs. Quantity

The practical demonstration of a simplified lifestyle may prove to be among the greatest gifts which Francis of Assisi made to humanity.

In the next thirty years, more new housing will be required, so economists predict, than has been built since time began. Ever scarcer materials will push housing costs through the roof until eventually millions may have no roofs at all.

Each individual in the world, some time in the future, will have to be content with less — simpler foods, smaller cars, less luxurious houses, more practical clothing, fewer luxuries.

Although he lived with meager material possessions, St. Francis embodied a life of joy. His example was extreme. A gradual simplification of lifestyles for everyone, however — whether he wishes it or not — may become the ultimate requirement as population doubles and triples.

Material resources are finite. Spiritual resources are infinite. Francis of Assisi demonstrated that greater dependence on the spirit, and less on materials, results in the greatest joy. His life confirmed that quality is more important than quantity.

A Patron Saint for Ecologists

The new theology of St. Francis, enunciated 800 years ago but only now finding ready takers, may be the world's only salvation. That is the opinion expressed by Lynn White, Jr., Professor of Medieval History at the University of California, Los Angeles, in a keynote address before the American Association for the Advancement of Science.

Drawing a word picture of the by-products of Western Science and Technology — among them smog, pollution, threat of genetic change from the bomb — that have gotten out of control and which threaten ecologic disaster, Prof. White told the assembled scientists: "I personally doubt that disastrous ecologic backlash can be avoided simply by applying to our problems more science and more technology. No creature other than man," he declares, "has ever managed to foul its nest in such short order."

Then Prof. White gave a statement which may one day prove to be world-shaking: "The remedy must . . . be essentially religious."

Prof. White indicts Judaeo-Christian theology for much of the mess we are in. According to that theology "Christianity not only established a dualism of man and nature but also insisted that it is God's will that man exploit nature for his own ends."

Prof. White states: "What we do about ecology depends on our ideas of the man-nature relationship. More science and more technology are not going to get us out of the present ecologic crisis until we find a new religion or rethink our old one."

"The present increasing disruption of the global environment," White told the scientists, "is the product of a dynamic technology and science that were originating in the same Western medieval world against which St. Francis was rebelling in so original a way. Their growth cannot be understood historically, apart from distinctive attitudes toward nature that are deeply grounded in Christian dogma . . . No new set of basic values has been accepted in our society to displace those of Christianity. Hence we shall continue to have a worsening ecologic crisis until we reject the Christian axiom that nature has no reason for existence save to serve man . . .

"Possibly we should ponder the greatest radical in Christian history since Christ, Saint Francis of Assisi.

"The greatest spiritual revolutionary in Western History, St. Francis proposed what he thought was an alternative Christian view of nature and man's relation to it: he tried to substitute the idea of the equality of all creatures including man, for the idea of man's limitless rule over creation. He failed. Both our present science and our present technology are so tinctured with orthodox Christian arrogance toward nature that no solution for our ecologic crisis can be expected from them alone. Since the roots of our trouble are so largely religious the remedy must also be essentially religious, whether we call it that or not. We must rethink and refeel our nature and destiny. The profoundly religious, but heretical, sense of the primitive Franciscans for the spiritual autonomy of all parts of nature may point a direction . . .

"**I Propose Francis As a Patron Saint For Ecologists.**"

Condensed from Prof. Lynn White, Jr.'s Address to the American Association for the Advancement of Science. 1966, by FRL & HL

Navajos walk in beauty.

Ecology and Brotherhood

More than 4000 miles separated Francis of Assisi from the big continent to be known as America. He never knew that the natives of that land believed as he did. How he would have rejoiced had he known.

Lame Deer said — "All living creatures are my relatives —
                    even a tiny bug."

Francis said — "All creatures, great and small, are brothers
                   and sisters to me."

Black Elk said — "When we use water . . . we should think of
                  the Great Spirit who is always flowing, giving
                  His power and life to everything."

Francis said — "Be praised, My Lord, through Sister Water, for
                  greatly useful, lowly, precious, chaste is she."

A wise saying of the Winnebago declared — "Holy Mother Earth,
                  the trees, and all nature, are witnesses of
                  your thoughts and deeds."

Francis said — "Be praised O Lord, through our Sister Mother Earth,
                  for she sustains and guides our life."

The Navajos chanted — "Beauty is before me,
                  Beauty is behind me. I walk in beauty."

St. Francis saw beauty in all of life.

The interdependence of all people is a part of the great fabric of life on this fragile planet Earth. These thoughts so eloquently echoed by our native American brothers, and by St. Francis, remind us to revere all creation.

Earth, Wind and Fire

Earth, Wind and Fire —
These three forces, large in the thoughts of St. Francis, inspire us
and fill us, too, with their power.

Earth

Who is not moved
by the beauty of the Earth?
New born each day,
Dew-drenched each night,
New yet old as time.
The Earth
Who feeds and governs us —
We love you!
Praise Be For Mother Earth!

Wind

Winds have blown over you for eons, O Earth —
Polishing and burnishing your rocks,
Carving arches and bridges with your power,
Driving countless vessels across the seas —
Turning windmills, creating energy —
Cooling the land, with gentle breezes,
Or lashing it with hurricane force.

Yet Brother Wind, how we love your sounds
In the trees, singing and sighing,
Whistling and whispering down the years,
Reviving us,
Yet leaving us in mystery.

The wind bloweth where it listeth —

We know not where it has gone.
Praise Be For Brother Wind!

Fire

Brother Fire, searing and scorching the Earth,
Yet warming us, as cold winds blow.
Who first rubbed stones together
To make you leap out and spark the wood,
To light and warm mankind?

Was it at dawn's first light
Or in Ice Age numbing cold?
O Prometheus, Fire Bringer, were you the first
To light the glow of embers?
Or some child in Egypt's land,
Playing with a mirror,
Catching the sun on papyrus,
Causing the sudden flame?

O Brother Fire, you who have been
Earth's vital energy for a million years,
Tell us your secret!
Praise Be For Brother Fire!

Living With St. Francis
Words of Personal Thanks

Francis of Assisi's influence on my life — and Helen's too — has been large.

An inborn love of Sister Mother Earth and all her creatures came from my parents and I probably received my name because of this. Forest-enclosed lakes and open fields, filled with the mysteries of birdsong, were my early playground; love of wildlife was my natural inheritance.

Around our home in rural Michigan, Miss Muffet would never have been frightened away by that spider. For us, the jingle went, rather, like this:

Little Miss Muffet sat on a tuffet,
Eating her curds and whey;
Along came a spider and sat down beside her,
AND THEY BOTH HAD A WONDERFUL DAY.

I, too, had wonderful days, in Michigan's mysterious woodlands although there was deep pain at times, as human crassness and cruelty became apparent to me as a child. Once I saw a hunter club a wounded cottontail to death. With set teeth I rushed home and next day that hunter's bloody club gave birth to a club of another kind, which a schoolmate and I founded to help protect wild animals.

When Helen and I were married we soon adopted a simplicity of lifestyle quite in contrast to that of most. How much Francis of Assisi influenced this we cannot say but, to the extent that he did, we are thankful for we were freed forever from competing with the Joneses.

California called us westward and our home, in time, became the chaparral-clothed acres containing the Eagle Rock, an historic 12-million-year-old natural landmark, where we created a bird and wildlife sanctuary. For construction purposes we used only materials which others had discarded as useless.

Our helper was Jan de Swart. Since then he has become an

internationally-known sculptor. Part of a patriarchal cedar pole —
castaway of the phone company — remained from our day's work
as we built a garden for birds.

With artisan's tools, Jan began shaping that humbled forest
monarch. Before our eyes emerged a stylized likeness of the Assisi
saint.

No statue sings the secrets of St. Francis in quite the manner
that this one does — its weathered age yet agelessness, the pat-
terned beauty of wormholes, some indentations made by a wood-
pecker, the texture which is soft but firm, the humble gentleness and
embedded love.

We have moved from Eagle Rock, as encroaching noise and
congestion frightened our wildlife away. St. Francis moved with
us. Now, in our garden overlooking the Pacific, he watches as
birds, and wild foxes, skunks, oppossums, raccoons — even an
occasional eagle — come to feed before his outstretched hand.

He whispers gently to the Capistrano swallows as they depart
southward every autumn. He greets them again in mid-March, even
before they return to nearby San Juan Capistrano Mission. The
Gambel Sparrows reverse this procedure. They leave our home to
fly northward, on almost the same day every April, and return
on regular schedule each September. St. Francis watches them
come and go. Our garden over which he presides is home not only
for birds which stay the year round but is a halfway station for
migrants from both hemispheres. He greets them all.

Helen and I migrate too. While we are away St. Francis —
with the help of our neighbors — watches after our birds. For
most of our lives, as makers of documentary educational films, we
have been travelers — but never tourists.

There is spiritual adventure in journeying the world with one
goal — one objective — in mind. Often we followed the by-lanes
of Europe — particularly Italy — with St. Francis as our unseen
guide. We searched our way from Key West to San Francisco in
the footsteps of the Franciscans. We followed him, and them, in
other areas of America and the world.

Treasures we never dreamed of poured into the storehouses of
our lives — treasures of physical discovery to begin with, as we
found new Francis of Assisi landmarks. Then treasures of the mind,
as our searches led us to new books about St. Francis which we
had never known before.

Inevitably there were new treasures of the spirit. One cannot
come under the spell of Assisi itself without growing spiritually. One
cannot live for months with Francis' Prayer, as we did while filming
SONG OF THE EARTH, without expanding in empathy and com-

Bird feeding time at the authors' wild life sanctuary,
Eagle Rock, California.

117

mitment to Jesus' two great commandments. One cannot know and live with the Assisi Saint, as it is necessary to do while writing about him and researching his life, without absorbing deep values in the process. As we grew to know St. Francis more and more, we grew to establish a far greater attachment to the one whose life he reflected — Jesus of Nazareth.

When we accepted an invitation from "Alive Now!" magazine to be guest editors and to write for a special issue on St. Francis, still more treasurers of the spirit showered our lives.

To know and love St. Francis is to grow, whether one starts the love affair as naturalist, ecologist, social activist, namesake, reformer, or deeply spiritual seeker. Francis of Assisi has added large frontiers to our lives, and new dimensions to our living. It is because we need to share these new frontiers and dimensions that we have written this book.

— FRANCIS R. LINE

POSTLUDE

MODERN SAINTS
CAN SAVE
OUR WORLD

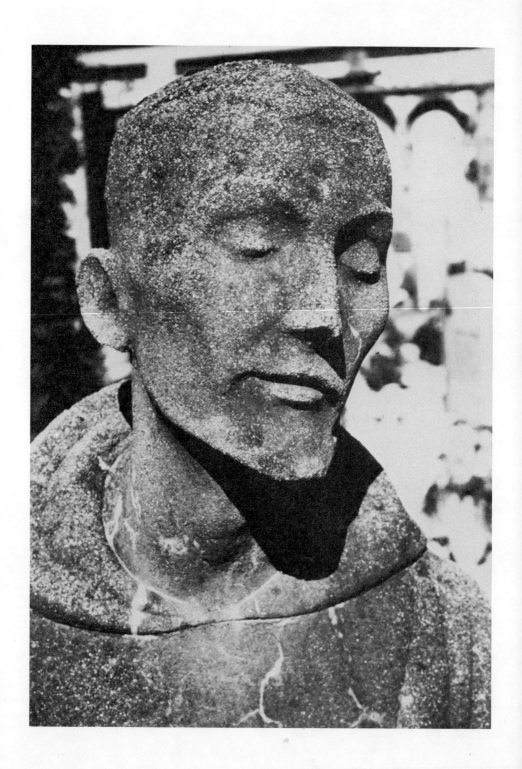

"Saints Alive!"

Twentieth century saints are in short supply. Yet they are needed at least as much as in the "Dark Ages." Practical, "ordinary" saints are especially needed, men and women who by example and creatively inspired lives can lead our world in the direction it needs to go if it is to survive.

Father James Keller caught a vision of this. Through the Christopher Movement, which he founded, common people in everyday life were instructed and inspired in achieving minor miracles. He said to them: "You can change the world." Many of them did — and are doing — just that.

Allan Hunter, in the selection of his which is included in the anthology, "Fellowship of the Saints," describes these world-shaking possibilities from a different approach. He relates how, during World War II, "in a special course of twenty-one days, a respectable citizen can be made over into a fighting fury, a commando unfailingly 'bloody-minded.' "

He then outlines ways in which, starting with much the same type of individuals but using a totally different approach with totally different goals, men and women can be brought up to serve their fellows through love and life rather than through hatred and death.

Pitirim Sorokin created the Harvard Research Center in Creative Altruism, and wrote a masterful 500-page study on this same subject — "The Ways and Power of Love." He opens up new vistas and new approaches through which individuals can turn their lives towards love and service. Saints, he implies, are not born; they are made.

The Franciscan followers of St. Francis, of course, have been practicing love for three-quarters of a millenium.

The process needs continual expansion. In this book we have chosen a different — and unconventional — approach, in the hope that it will reach readers who are new to many of St. Francis' concepts but are open to fresh breezes of the spirit.

Many people believe that sainthood is impossible, or even undesirable. This may be due to a lack of understanding of what a saintly life is or can be. Anyone who sings St. Francis' Song — not alone with his lips but with his life — is a saintly person. Anyone who prays St. Francis' Prayer — not just with phrases but with motivated feeling — that person is doing a saint's work.

We have described how Francis **lived** his Song into reality. We can well close our little volume with a final portrayal of the St. Francis Prayer, and show how all of us can crystallize its concepts into Christ-inspired 20th Century living. In a few years we shall enter the 21st Century. At 21, one is supposed to have grown up, to have become of age, to be an adult. The world, thus, has only a few years to achieve a maturity for which it has long been struggling. The sincere living of St. Francis' Prayer can aid in that achievement.

The Prayer's opening consists of eight mighty steps on the ladder to maturity. The first two, taken together, are perhaps the most important:

Where there is hatred, let me put love,
Where there is anger, let me put forgiveness.

The most important place to start renewing the world is in the home and in one's immediate surroundings. "Afghanistanism" is a term applied to those who see the need of change in remote countries but overlook any need of renewal in themselves. Hatreds and resentments may well exist in Afghanistan but they are also the ingredients of broken homes and lives in Anytown, U.S.A. **Our** lives. **Our** homes. **Our** towns.

Love and forgiveness are merely words. But they represent mighty concepts — mighty **healing** concepts — when they're **used.** Saintliness consists in practicing, not just preaching, forgiveness. When elements of hatred, anger, and resentment begin to flare in a situation, an attitude of complete forgiveness — on the part of anyone involved — can begin changing the atmosphere. As greater unity develops, love and respect return.

Those who simply give lip service to St. Francis' Prayer are parrots; to change the world, to change our homes, to change ourselves, we must give **life** service to the concept.

After that, we will all be better qualified to tackle problems in Afghanistan.

Where there is discord, let me put unity.

These gentle words from the St. Francis Prayer can profitably head the agenda for every conference table, board meeting, church committee session — for every group where plans are being made or differences being discussed.

The key word is "me." As each individual — not the other

person — seeks to erase discords and strives for unity, creative results can, and do, come forth.

Where there is doubt, let me put faith.

Faith is needed by a worshiper in church. It is needed, also, by a person trying to tackle a difficult task, solve a hard problem, raise a family, or achieve a respectable life.

When faith wavers, or doubt arises, the prayerful repetition of this phrase will help. Then the taking of a step forward — just one step to begin with — can start one on the upward road.

Where there is error, let me put truth.

This one concept can renew society, physically, intellectually, and spiritually. Consider the value of this concept, in world-changing potential, for those responsible for children's television programs, especially TV commercials — from the highest company executives to the lowest paid writers. The deep significance of what it would mean to replace error with truth on the airwaves can scarcely be overemphasized. Children's programming can become a strong factor in enhancing, rather than destroying, the finest physical, mental, and spiritual qualities of childhood.

Replace error with truth. What a concept for every author, for all advertisers, for those who write and edit the daily news.

The concept of replacing error with truth, applied to the construction of an automobile, or bicycle, or any mechanical device, can result in a product in which safety, beauty, and utility are built-in. Such a concept can lead to a new era in business ethics where profit goes hand-in-hand with quality.

Replace error with truth. In the treatment of one's own body — in determining what we shall eat, or inhale, or sniff, or drink — we can opt for the true or the false, the helpful or the harmful.

This one concept, intelligently followed, can raise all of life to a higher plane.

Where there is despair, let me bring happiness.

Francis of Assisi's lifelong ministry of love began with an act of turning despair into hope — he kissed a leper. If we go out today and figuratively kiss a leper, we too are dispelling despair. It can be by speaking a word of needed cheer or encouragement, making a phone call to someone in distress, writing a letter to relieve anxiety, doing an act of real charity. It is a solid fact that "kissing a leper" can be a more generous act than giving a million dollars. Few of us are millionaries, but all of us know how to kiss.

Where there is sadness, let me bring joy.

Once, when her whole household was gloomy, a mother quietly began to hum a simple tune. After a bit, she started singing the words. One of the youngsters, almost unconsciously, caught up the refrain. Then another. Within an hour, although no one really knew what had happened, the whole household was joyous.

St. Francis sang and lived a Song — which changed the world. Even the least of us can start humming some simple tune.

Where there is darkness, let me bring light.

The one hundred thousand persons filling every seat of the Rose Bowl in Pasadena were asked by the announcer to participate in an experiment. The electric floodlights were turned off so that complete darkness swallowed up the entire stadium. Each person had been given a match and cautioned to use it with care.

"Now," said the announcer, "each of you light your match."

One hundred thousand flames —each one tiny in itself — instantly spread light to every corner of the great arena.

All of us are participants in the world's arena. Each of us has a light, small to be sure, but mightily effective when combined with the light of others in the areas close about us.

It is in giving that we receive;
In forgiving that we obtain forgiveness;
In dying that we rise to eternal life.
As we die to ourselves, miracles of love begin to happen.
SAINTS ALIVE!

Francis Raymond Line and Helen E. Line

About the Authors

Francis and Helen Line, both together and separately, have written for **National Geographic Magazine, Arizona Highways, Boys' Life, Wide World of England,** and have lectured with films at Constitution Hall in Washington, Town Hall and Columbia University in New York, Carnegie Hall in Pittsburgh, Orchestra Hall and Field Museum in Chicago, The Denver Natural History Museum, and similar places nationwide. To most of these places Francis has returned as many as a dozen times over a 25 year period, having appeared personally before more than a million persons.

Mr. and Mrs. Line presented their film on St. Francis before the Forum of the First United Nations Conference on the Human Environment at Stockholm, in 1972.

Their book, **Blueprint For Living,** was published by The Upper Room of Nashville. The Upper Room has also published their small book, **Our Road To Prayer,** part of a special prayer series.

The Lines regularly attend and/or lead Disciplined Order of Christ Retreats. Helen is a National Board member of the Disciplined Order of Christ, and a past president and present Board member of its Western Region. Francis is a University of Michigan graduate, magna cum laude, a member of Phi Beta Kappa, Los Angeles Adventurers' Club, among other groups.

The Lines carry on an extensive lay ministry of service in their local community and church, as well as serving on the Board of the Watts area YMCA. On January 15, 1975, the Los Angeles Metropolitan YMCA presented the first Martin Luther King, Jr. Human Dignity Award to Mr. and Mrs. Line, in recognition of outstanding service rendered to the youth of Watts.

There's A Chance For Us!

You're a saint
If you get listed in a sacred calendar,
Or get leaded into a stained glass window.
These are two ways of achieving sainthood —
But there are others.

You can stop to aid a person in distress,
Say a kind word to the harried waitress or clerk,
Sing a song over a sink full of dishes,
Or an office desk groaning with memos.
You can speak up when speaking is needed,
And keep silent when silence is healing.
You can give a smile,
Say THANK YOU,
Offer a word of needed praise,
Perform an act of kindness,
Be gentle.

By word and action,
You can spread God's message of love!

If you do such things now and then,
You are human.
If they become your lifestyle
You have planted the seeds of sainthood,
    Whether or not you ever get listed in a sacred calendar,
    Or get leaded into a stained glass window.

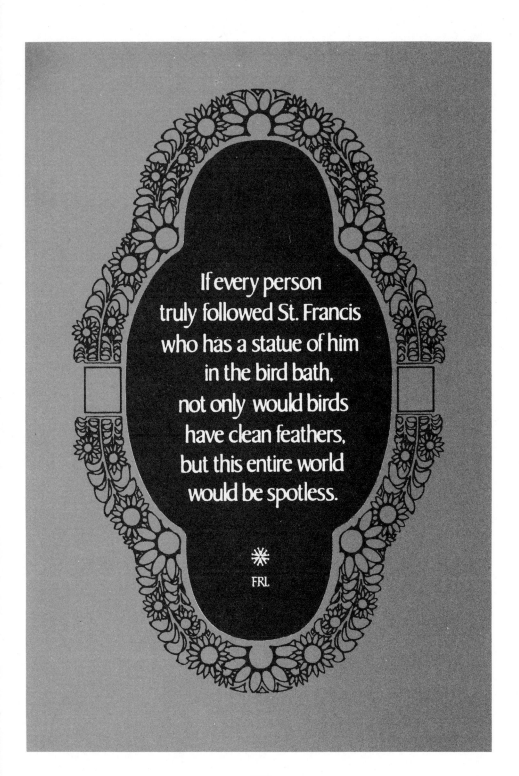

If every person
truly followed St. Francis
who has a statue of him
in the bird bath,
not only would birds
have clean feathers,
but this entire world
would be spotless.

FRL

127